D0041883

# THE TRUTH ABOUT CHRISTMAS

## ITS TRADITIONS UNRAVELLED

Philip Ardagh writes both fiction and non-fiction, and is a familiar face at book festivals in England, Scotland and Wales. His books have been translated into numerous languages, including Latin.

THE TRUTH ABOUT CHRISTMAS

PHILIP ARDAGH

ITS TRADITIONS UNRAVELLED

Illustrated by Marian Hill

MACMILLAN CHILDREN'S BOOKS

First published 2001 by Macmillan Children's Books

This edition published 2012 by Macmillan Children's Books
a division of Pan Macmillan Limited
20 New Wharf Road, London N1 9RR
Basingstoke and Oxford
Associated companies throughout the world
www.panmacmillan.com

ISBN 978-1-4472-0167-0

Text copyright © Philip Ardagh 2001
Illustrations copyright © Marian Hill 2001

1 3 5 7 9 8 6 4 2

A CIP catalogue record for this book is available from the British Library.
Printed and bound by CPI Group (UK) Ltd, Croydon CR0 4YY

*For my parents,*
*Christopher and Rosemary,*
*who made my childhood*
*Christmases so magical*

*Forth to the wood did merry-men go,*
*To gather in the mistletoe.*

From *Old Christmas*
– Walter Scott (1771–1832)

# Contents

25 December     1

The Christmas Tree     5

Father Christmas     9

Hanging Up Stockings     14

Coming Down the Chimney     16

The Flying Reindeer     17

The Fairy at the Top of the Tree     20

The Star     22

The Yule Log     23

Holly and Ivy     26

The Flowering Hawthorn     29

The Christmas Rose     33

Candles     35

Advent Calendars     37

Turkey Dinner     38

Sprouts!     41

Mince Pies                    43

Christmas Pudding             45

Robin Red Breast              50

Christmas Cards               53

Christmas Carols              57

Wassailing                    62

Christmas Crackers            66

The Christmas Crib            70

Mistletoe                     74

Boxing Day                    77

Christmas Presents            79

Twelfth Night                 81

Pantomimes                    83

Scrooge                       84


Index                         86

# 25 December

FOR CHRISTIANS, CHRISTMAS Day is a celebration of the birth of Jesus Christ, the son of God. In the West, this is celebrated on 25 December, but this date wasn't really thought to be Christ's birthday. No Bible scholar really believes that Jesus was actually born in a stable in Bethlehem on the 25th, so how did this date come about?

The answer has much to do with another sun, this time of the 's-u-n', rather than the 's-o-n', variety. Long before 25 December became Christmas Day, it was a special date in the Roman calendar. There was a festival to celebrate the sun called Saturnalia and, in the middle of it was the 25th: *Dies Natalis Solis Invicti* (the Birthday of the Invincible One). This was all a part of what is called the winter solstice, the period when the shortest day and the longest night are followed by longer, brighter, warmer days.

In celebration, people decorated their houses and presents were exchanged. Sound familiar?

## An emperor's decree

When the Roman emperor Constantine became the first Christian emperor, he declared that it would be Christ's birthday that was celebrated on 25 December instead. The non-Christian Romans didn't mind. They still had an excuse for a party. What we don't know is exactly when this first 25 December Christmas was actually celebrated, but it had become an event by AD 354.

## Christmas ups and downs

Christmas hasn't always been celebrated in Britain since then. In 1647, Oliver Cromwell's Puritan parliament abolished Christmas altogether! After the execution of King Charles I, Cromwell ruled the country. He believed that to be a Christian you must lead a serious, sensible and simple life full of prayer. Puritanism had no room for joyful festivities and feasts.

In 1660, with a king back on the English throne, Christmas was reinstated but, by the 1790s, the idea had simply fizzled out! In Britain, it wasn't until around the time that Charles Dickens published his story *A Christmas Carol*, in 1843, that Christmas came back with a bang. Since then, it's been one of the most important dates in the year!

## Some other confusions over dates

In the Christian calendar, a date marked BC means 'Before Christ' and AD means '*Anno Domini*' which is Latin for 'in the year of our Lord' (i.e. after His birth). What makes it confusing, though, is that most historians now believe that Jesus Christ was probably born in what we call 6 BC. In other words, Christ himself was born six years 'Before Christ'!

# The Christmas Tree

IN WINTER, WHEN most trees are bare, fir trees are covered in bright green needles. By bringing them into the house, we're bringing in a little feeling of new growth and summer. By decorating the tree with tinsel and baubles we're adding blossom and fruit. But when did the idea of chopping down a tree, bringing it into the home and decorating it begin?

Well – pardon the pun – it obviously had its roots in earlier pagan (non-Christian) celebrations but, according to the historian Clement A. Miles, the first recorded mention of a Christmas tree was in 1605 in

Strasbourg. It was covered in everything from paper roses to sweets and gold foil.

## The three points

To justify having what was, probably, originally part of a pagan festival as the centre of Christian celebrations, the Christmas tree has since been given added Christian symbolism. It was pointed out that the basic shape of a Christmas tree is a triangle, with one point at the top. The three points are said to represent the 'Holy Trinity' of God the Father, God the Son and God the Holy Ghost.

## St Boniface

According to legend, in eighth-century Germany, a Christian saint called Boniface stumbled upon a group of pagans worshipping an oak tree. They were just about to sacrifice a baby to the tree when St Boniface dashed to his rescue. He snatched the axe about to be used in the sacrifice, and chopped down the tree instead. Picking up the baby, Boniface saw that there, growing between the roots of the chopped-down oak, was a tiny fir tree. To him, this symbolized new life coming from death, as with Christ's resurrection. From then on, the tree became an important part of Christmas celebrations in Germany.

## The first tree in England

Many people believe that the idea of the Christmas tree was brought over to England by Prince Albert, the German husband of Queen Victoria. Albert first ordered a tree from Coburg in Christmas 1841.

In fact, there had already been a Christmas tree at Windsor Castle in the 1790s. It had been ordered by Queen Charlotte, the wife of King George III.

However, it was Prince Albert's tree that somehow caught the public imagination and made the Christmas tree such an important part of Christmas in Britain.

## The Trafalgar Square tree

One of the most famous Christmas trees is the one presented to the British people every year by Norway. This is as a 'thank you' to Britain for its help during the Second World War. When Norway was occupied by enemy forces, the King of Norway, King Haakon, escaped to England. Here, he set up a 'Free Norwegian Government'. Since 1947, a tree about 23 metres (70 feet) tall has been sent over from Oslo and erected in Trafalgar Square, near Nelson's Column, every Christmas.

# Father Christmas

IF CHRISTMAS DAY is supposed to celebrate the birth of Christ, where does Father Christmas fit into all of this? Why does he choose Christmas Eve to bring children presents?

The clue lies in his other name: Santa Claus. This means 'Saint Claus' and is short for Saint Nicholas. Saint Nicholas – before he became a saint – was a bishop in Myra (in what is now Turkey). He was born around AD 270 and became well-known for giving gifts to the poor anonymously. (He didn't leave a note or stay around for the 'thank yous'.) He often slipped into their homes at night, leaving gifts in shoes or stockings . . . or so the story goes. Once, taking pity on a poor father and his three hungry daughters, he threw three purses, bulging with gold, into their house. Over time, news of his good deeds came out. What better person to distribute presents come Christmas time, as a celebration of peace and goodwill?

## Kris Kringle

Father Christmas goes by many different names in different countries. The German for 'Christ child' is 'Christkindl' which soon became Kris Kringle, another of Santa's nicknames! Most are variations of Santa Claus, however (Sinter Klaas, in the Netherlands, for example) or Father Christmas (Père Noël, in France).

## That red suit

Though few people have been lucky enough to meet him, we all know that Father Christmas – or Santa Claus if you prefer – is fat, jolly, has a white beard, and wears a red suit . . . but why a *red* suit? The Coca-Cola company – yes, the same people who make the fizzy drink – claim that they gave Santa the image of the red suit in 1931, when Haddon Sundblom drew Father Christmas wearing one in one of their advertisements. The suit was the same colour as the Coke logo.

Although this 1931 advertisement may have made red the most popular colour for Father Christmas to be shown wearing, pictures of him wearing a red suit had, the truth be told, appeared before then. It is even referred to in a book from 1821. But there are old pictures of him in green suits too.

## Santa's little helpers

Father Christmas doesn't only go by different names in different countries, he also gets up to different things. In Britain and America, he flies around in a sleigh pulled by magic reindeer on Christmas Eve (24 December), so that children wake up on Christmas morning to find he's left them presents; often in stockings or pillow cases.

Many of the toys he brings are made or collected by an army of helpers – usually elves – who help to pack his sack.

In the Netherlands, Father Christmas delivers the presents on 5 December. He used to have a friend with him called Black Peter. While Santa gave presents to the good children, Black Peter whipped the bad ones. Today, fortunately, Santa travels round Holland on his own. In Germany, though, the presents are delivered by Knecht Ruprecht, who wears clothes of animal skins and straw.

## The Santa we know today

What we now know about Father Christmas, or Santa Claus, owes much to the Americans of the nineteenth century. In a poem written in 1822, often referred to as *The Night Before Christmas*, but originally titled A *Visit from St Nicholas*, the journalist Clement Clarke Moore describes the 'jolly old elf' in great detail, from his plump tummy, white beard and twinkling eyes to the soot on his clothes and the sack of presents on his back.

A year earlier, a book had been published in America called *The Children's Friend*, which described his red costume and magical ability of covering such huge distances in just one night. Even earlier than that, in 1809, the American writer Washington Irving (probably most famous today for having written *The Legend of Sleepy Hollow*) wrote *Father Knickerbocker's History of New York*. This includes reports of Santa riding over the rooftops in his sleigh and delivering presents to good children.

Finally, between 1860 and 1881, the American illustrator Thomas Nast drew a whole series of pictures of Santa, including his workshop at the North Pole.

Whether any of these men ever actually met Father Christmas or whether they were working on information from other eye witnesses, their images are the ones with the most influence on how we imagine Father Christmas to look.

# Hanging Up Stockings

WHEN SAINT NICHOLAS was a bishop in Myra, he used to leave gifts for the poor. Often, he would slip into their houses unseen at night and hide the presents of food or money. He would throw gifts through an open window or, perhaps, even down a chimney.

According to legend, one of Saint Nicholas's favourite hiding places for gifts was in shoes or stockings. Why? Because he knew that people would put their feet in them first thing in the morning. That way they'd be sure to find what he had left them. When Saint Nicholas became Santa

Claus, or Father Christmas, he still liked filling stockings, so children learned to leave them out for him to find.

Because most houses were warmed by fires most had chimneys, and that was the quickest way for him to get inside. That's why most stockings used to be hung on the chimney breast. Today, people often leave their stockings – or empty pillow cases – at the foot of the bed.

*'Twas the night before Christmas,*
*when all through the house*
*Not a creature was stirring, not even a*
*mouse:*
*The stockings were hung by the*
*chimney with care,*
*In the hope that St Nicholas soon*
*would be there . . .*

From *A Visit from St Nicholas*
– Clement Clarke Moore (1779–1863)

15

# Coming Down the Chimney

FATHER CHRISTMAS PROBABLY started coming down chimneys early in the nineteenth century when most houses still had working fireplaces. Delivering presents on a sleigh pulled by flying reindeer meant that rooftops were the easiest place to land and chimneys the quickest way into locked houses. Today, of course, he often uses other magical methods to get inside. Chimneys aren't compulsory.

During pre-Christian winter rituals in Germany, the goddess Hertha was thought to come down the chimney to reward the good and punish the bad.

# The Flying Reindeer

IN THE MYTHS and legends of the old Norse ('North') countries of Scandinavia, many of their heroes and gods travelled across the skies in flying chariots. Thor, the god of thunder, had a chariot pulled by two massive goats. Their hoofs cracked the sky with sparks of lightning and the sounds of thunder. Legend had it that they caused all storms!

In the Scandinavian countries of Norway, Iceland and Greenland, many people got around by reindeer and sleigh. It makes sense, therefore, for Father Christmas to use reindeer in the frozen north where he lives, and for them to fly, in order to speed him on his way. The earliest reference to Father Christmas getting around by this mode of transport dates back to the early nineteenth century.

But what about Rudolph the red-nosed reindeer and the names of all those other reindeer? It's a bit like trying to remember the name of the seven dwarfs in Walt Disney's *Snow White*.

Rudolph first appeared in an advertisement for the Montgomery Ward department store in Chicago, USA, in 1939. Every child who visited the store's Santa was given a free booklet containing a poem about Rudolph written by Robert L. May. Over 2.4 million booklets were eventually given away.

In 1949, a friend of Mr May's called Johnny Marks set the poem to music. It was recorded by the then-superstar Gene Autry, 'the singing cowboy'. *Rudolph the Red-Nosed Reindeer* became one of the best-selling records of all time, has been re-recorded by hundreds of different artists and has sold more than 80 million records!

The eight other reindeer are: Dasher, Dancer, Prancer, Vixen, Comet, Cupid, Donder and Blitzen, though Donder is usually called 'Donner' these days.

They first appeared in the famous poem by the American Clement Clarke Moore, originally entitled *A Visit From St Nicholas*.

(By the way, Disney's seven dwarfs were: Happy, Sleepy, Grumpy, Sneezy, Doc, Dopey and – the one most people forget, poor fella – Bashful.)

# The Fairy at the Top of the Tree

OF COURSE, THE thing about the fairy at the top of the Christmas tree is that it isn't supposed to be a fairy at all but an angel. There are many angels in the Bible and, in the nativity story, the Angel of the Lord appears before the shepherds to tell them of Christ's birth.

You can see how the confusion came about, though. Both angels and fairies have wings. Many Christmas traditions have their roots in pagan rituals, so some people ended up calling the angel a fairy!

This does, of course, make one wonder whether fairy lights – also used to decorate the tree – should really be called 'angel lights'.

*While shepherds watched their flocks by*
  *night,*
*All seated on the ground,*
*The Angel of the Lord came down,*
*And glory shone around.*
*'Fear not,' said he, for mighty dread*
*Had seized their troubled mind;*
*'Glad tidings of great joy I bring*
*To you and all mankind.'*

From *While Shepherds*
*Watched Their Flocks*
– Nahum Tate (1652–1715)

# The Star

THE STAR AT the top of a Christmas tree represents the star which, according to the Bible, appeared above the stable in Bethlehem where Christ was born. One theory is that the 'star' was really a bright comet, but astronomers have no records of any being around at the time of Christ's birth.

If Christ was born in 6 BC (*see page 4*) then the planets Mars, Jupiter and Saturn were in a strange configuration. This could have been the mysterious sign that the three wise men saw in the sky, which led them on their hunt for Jesus.

# The Yule Log

THE NEAREST MANY people get to having a yulc log in the house today is by making or buying the chocolate variety (a bit like a Swiss roll coated in chocolate streaked to look like bark, perhaps with the finishing touch of a sprig of holly on top). A real yule log is a real log . . . and it's on fire too. But what does it have to do with Christmas?

As a celebration of the birth of Christ, nothing. As part of a very ancient winter tradition, plenty.

Some Christmas cards still include the words 'yuletide greetings', and 'yuletide' has come to mean Christmas, but what

THE TRUTH ABOUT CHRISTMAS

did 'yule' originally mean?

Most experts seem to agree that it comes from the Anglo-Saxon word *hwéol*, meaning 'wheel'. This probably refers to the sun, moving through certain 'wheeling points', which were special dates in the calendar, mapped out on charts. As discussed back on pages 1–2, 25 December was an important pagan sun festival long before it became Christmas Day.

The chief of the Norse gods, Odin, was called 'Jul-Vatter', or 'Yule-father', because he was strongly associated with the sun. Scandinavians used to celebrate the 'Jul' or Yule festival in what is now Christmas time.

Now, back to the log itself. The Celts believed that, for twelve days at the end of December, the sun stood still (which is why the days grew shorter and shorter). If they could keep yule logs burning bright for those twelve days, then the sun would be persuaded to move again, and make the days grow longer. If a yule log went out, then there could be terrible bad luck.

In the days when people still had large fireplaces, a yule log was dragged in on Christmas Eve. It was lit with a piece of the old yule log kept from the year before – so the logs were connected in this manner, way, way back down the years. The Victorians made sure that theirs stayed alight for twelve hours, instead of days.

*Come, bring with a noise,*
*My merry, merry boys,*
*The Christmas log to the firing.*

From *Ceremonies for Christmas*
– Robert Herrick (1591–1674)

# Holly and Ivy

WHAT HOLLY AND ivy instantly have in common is that they're evergreen. When other plants lose their leaves in winter, both holly and ivy keep theirs. If people wanted to bring colour and growth into their houses at winter, then these were the obvious choice. They came to represent the promise of everlasting life and the coming of spring. An obvious religious connection is that Christ, too, offers everlasting life.

One of the more common Christmas traditions is that the prickles on the holly leaves represent the crown of thorns Christ wore on the cross. The holly's red berries represent His drops of blood. The Christmas wreath, which often includes holly, also has connotations of both death and rebirth.

## Who rules the house?

One strange tradition is that holly represents the man of the house (the husband) and ivy the woman (the wife). If holly is brought into the house first at Christmas – which mustn't be done before Christmas Eve – the man will be 'head of the house' and in charge for the following year. If ivy is brought in first, this will be the woman's role.

## Prophetic powers

Holly is traditionally said to be hated by witches, but does have some magic uses. Pick nine smooth holly leaves, tie them with nine knots into a handkerchief and put the bundle under your pillow. What you dream that night should be a prophecy of things to come . . . if you believe in that kind of thing!

## Bad luck

People used to be reluctant to throw holly and ivy away once they had been used as decorations. This was bad luck. They were either fed to animals or burnt. It was also considered very bad luck if so much as a single holly or ivy leaf fell to the floor when taking your decorations down.

> *The holly and the ivy*
> *When they are all full-grown*
> *Of all the trees that are in the wood*
> *The holly bears the crown.*

From *The Holly and the Ivy*
– Traditional

# The Flowering Hawthorn

ACCORDING TO THE Bible, when Christ was taken down from the cross, a man named Joseph of Arimathea had His body put in his own tomb. It was from this tomb that Christ rose from the dead.

According to legend, Joseph of Arimathea came to England many years later. He thrust his large wooden staff – a kind of walking stick – into the ground on Wearyall Hill in Glastonbury. It immediately grew roots and branches and became a hawthorn bush. Thereafter, every Christmas Eve, it suddenly burst into blossom.

THE TRUTH ABOUT CHRISTMAS

## A change in the calendar

In 1752, the British calendar was put back so that the date in Britain would be the same as in the rest of Europe. This meant that, although Christmas was celebrated on the same calendar date as before, it wasn't on the same actual day.

Apparently, Joseph of Arimathea's hawthorn bush kept on blossoming on the *old* Christmas Eve. (It was now twelve days out from the new one!) Some people argued, therefore, that the old date must be the true anniversary of the birth of Christ and that the new calendar was wrong.

## Destroyed!

In the seventeenth century, Cromwell's Puritans uprooted and destroyed what had now become known as the Glastonbury Thorn. Luckily, people had taken cuttings from the thorn over the years, so it lived on. One such cutting grew into the bush at the ruins of Glastonbury Abbey. Another is said to thrive in Orcop in Herefordshire.

## Other Christmas thorns

Throughout the country, there were a number of 'special' thorns that were said to blossom on Christmas Day (by the old calendar). One such bush was in Quainton, Buckinghamshire. When the new calendar was enforced, and Christmas fell early in 1752, two thousand people gathered around the shrub. As with the Glastonbury Thorn, the buds didn't open. This was also taken as a sign that the new Christmas Day wasn't Christmas Day at all . . . that it must still fall on the 'new' 5 January.

## A simple explanation

In winter when most trees were bare (and fewer exotic plants had been imported from abroad), a flowering hawthorn must have been an impressive sight. Winter-flowering hawthorns actually flower – come into blossom – twice a year. For them to have opened their buds on, or around, Christmas Day must have added to their importance, which is why these stories grew up around them.

*For ev'ry shrub, and ev'ry blade of
    grass,
And ev'ry pointed thorn, seem'd
    wrought in glass;
In pearls and rubies rich the
    hawthorns show,
While thro' the ice the crimson berries
    glow.*

From *A Winter Piece*
– Ambrose Philips (1674–1749)

# The Christmas Rose

AFTER THE ANGEL Gabriel had appeared before the shepherds on the hillside, and told them of the birth of the Baby Jesus in a stable in Bethlehem, he showed them the way by walking on foot. The shepherds brought the gift of a lamb with them, but a little girl who joined them on their journey had nothing to give. The Angel Gabriel touched the ground with his staff, and a beautiful rose grew out of the earth. The little girl picked the rose and gave it to Jesus in His crib. Or so says one traditional French tale.

Another version tells how each shepherd

brought a separate gift to the Baby Jesus, but one had nothing to give. He did not want to go into the stable empty-handed, so he plucked a simple daisy along the way. It had a yellow centre and pure white petals. When the shepherd offered it to the Christ Child, the Baby touched the daisy to His lips, and the edge of each petal turned rose red. Look closely, and you'll see that all daisies are now tinged with red. Perhaps they represent the blood of Christ.

The Christmas rose is also white, and often tinged with red, and is still put in a vase and prominently displayed by many, come Christmas time.

> *There is no rose of such virtue*
> *As is the rose that bare Jesu.*
> *Alleluia*

From *The Rose*
– Anonymous, fifteenth century

# Candles

IN THE DAYS long before electricity, candles were the main source of light in most homes. In Victorian times, tiny candles were placed on Christmas trees to make them look even more magical (whereas, today, most of us use fairy lights).

The biggest danger was the candle tipping over and setting fire to the pine needles and decorations.

Candle wax also dripped down on to the candle-holders and splattered on to the floor. Spiral candles were invented so that the wax would run slowly down the grooves and not drip.

As more and more homes got electricity, the demand for candles fell. As a treat, people would buy candles to use in candlesticks on the dinner table on Christmas Day. Often they were red, and often spiral too.

Today, candles are very much in fashion, with whole shops given over to selling all the different varieties. People use candles all the year round, not because they need to see by them, but for the pleasure of it.

There is a candle still special to Christmas though: the advent candle, with rings around it numbered 1 to 24, representing Advent.

# Advent Calendars

OLDER PEOPLE OFTEN complain that they don't like these 'new-fangled' advent calendars with chocolates behind each door, but prefer the traditional ones that simply have pictures.

In truth, the earliest advent calendars all contained chocolates and little presents! The first calendars were made in Germany at the end of the nineteenth century. These advent calendars were much bigger than today's, but still had twenty-four numbered doors. Advent is simply the period in December leading up to Christmas.

# Turkey Dinner

WHAT COULD BE more traditional than a roast turkey for Christmas? That's a tricky one to answer because, although turkeys have been around for a long while, their popularity has gone up and down when it comes to Christmas.

Turkeys come from North America, where they used to run wild. The first European settlers there found that they were a plentiful supply of meat. This is why a turkey dinner is a traditional part of the Thanksgiving Day celebrations, each November, in the United States.

In medieval England, peacocks and swans

were eaten by the rich at Christmas, but boar's head was the main course. In the eighteenth century, turkey, along with beef, slowly replaced boar's head as most people's Christmas meal in Britain, not least because wild boar were very rare. By Victorian times, people were usually eating either turkey or goose at Christmas.

In Dickens's short novel *A Christmas Carol*, the character Scrooge has a boy fetch a prize turkey from a shop window on Christmas morning. In the Sherlock Holmes story *The Blue Carbuncle*, by Sir Arthur Conan Doyle, however, the blue carbuncle – a gem – is hidden in the crop (neck) of a goose from a 'goose club'. People joined such clubs to give regular payments to save up for their goose at Christmas.

Over time, as more and more turkeys were farmed in Britain, and freezing and packaging methods improved, people began to switch from goose to turkey, come Christmas. Why? Because the meat wasn't so rich and fatty, and you could get much more from a single bird.

And where did the tradition of cranberry sauce come from? Also America. As well as wild turkeys, there was a plentiful supply of wild cranberries too!

> *Christmas is coming, the goose is*
> *getting fat,*
> *Please to put a penny in the old*
> *man's hat . . .*

– Traditional, English

# Sprouts!

THE ONE PART of the Christmas meal that lots and lots of children seem to hate is Brussel sprouts, but they're still a must for most people's Christmas Day! Children can't imagine why on earth any grown-up in his or her right mind would choose to eat them, but that's because sprouts really do taste more bitter to children. As we grow older, our taste buds develop. In other words, sprouts taste better as you get older. It's true!

Some people only have sprouts at Christmas, so there's some confusion about preparing them.

You're supposed to cut a cross with a knife on the bottom of each sprout before putting it in the water to boil. Some people assume that the 'X' is for Xmas, or has something to do with Christ being put on the cross. In fact, the cross is cut on the hardest part of the sprout – the stalk – to help it soften more easily when it cooks!

But why eat sprouts in the first place? Today, when nowhere in the world is more than twenty-four hours away, vegetables can be 'in season' all the year round. They're simply flown in from abroad, or grown under special conditions. In the old days, you could only eat fresh winter vegetables in winter . . . and sprouts were just about perfect around Christmas time. People were eating them way back in the 1580s.

# 𝔐ince 𝔓ies

MINCE PIES HAVE been a part of Christmas fayre for a long time, but have been through two major changes. The first is their shape. What originally made mince pies a traditional part of Christmas was that they were baked to look like Christ's crib. By the 1600s, some cooks were even adding little pastry Baby Jesuses! The pies were eventually banned, along with the celebration of Christmas Day itself, by Oliver Cromwell's parliament (*see page 3*).

People still wanted to eat mince pies, of course, so they simply made them round. When Oliver Cromwell died and a king was back on the throne, Christmas was celebrated once more, but mince pies kept their new round shape.

Then came the second change. Mince pies used to contain minced meat as well as the fruit and spices. Gradually, people started leaving the minced meat out until, by Victorian times, they were the fruit pies we know today.

Today, some people leave out a mince pie for Father Christmas to eat when he's left your presents. Other traditions say that you can make a wish when you take your first bite of mince pie at Christmas . . . and it's supposed to be bad luck not to eat a mince pie someone offers you!

# Christmas Pudding

NOWADAYS, MOST CHRISTMAS puddings are the shape of the upturned basin – often plastic – that they're steamed, boiled or microwaved in. Yet pictures of traditional Christmas puddings often show them as round as a football! So why were they made in this shape . . . and how?

To answer that, we need to go back even further to when the Christmas pud began life as a Christmas porridge called frumenty. Instead of eating it at the end of a big Christmas meal, this porridge was eaten in the lead-up to the Christmas Day feast. It was a 'fasting meal', designed to leave plenty of room in the tummy for all those up-coming Christmas goodies.

Frumenty was made up of raisins, currants, spices, wines and boiling beef and mutton (for the fat).

Over time, frumenty had more and more ingredients added to it, making it stiffer and stiffer and more pudding-like: eggs, breadcrumbs, dried fruits, ales (beers) and spirits. By 1595, it was a plum pudding, served at the end of the Christmas meal . . .

. . . just in time to be banned by Oliver Cromwell's Puritans as 'unfit for God-fearing people'.

## The Pudding King

It was King George I who made Christmas pudding popular again in 1714. He even had the nickname of 'the Pudding King'. (He did love his food.) A story grew up that he'd actually 'invented' Christmas pudding, but in fact he'd simply rediscovered it, 'fine-tuned' it and put it firmly back on the Christmas menu.

## Round like a cannonball

Once all these ingredients had been mixed together, they needed to be kept in place when cooked. Back in Tudor times, they were wrapped in pig's gut before being boiled, and came out like a big sausage (rather like haggis wrapped in sheep's stomach).

As time went on, the ingredients were rolled into a big ball and wrapped up in a hessian cloth to form a bag, before being lowered into the water for boiling . . . and that's why they came out a beautiful round shape. In other words, its shape had to do with the cooking method rather than any particular symbolic significance.

## Stir-Up Sunday

A number of traditions have grown up around preparing Christmas puddings, if you make your own. Some say that the pudding should be made by the 25th Sunday after Trinity. Others say that it should be made on the last Sunday before Advent, known as 'Stir-Up Sunday'.

You'd be forgiven for thinking it's called Stir-Up Sunday because that's when the pudding's ingredients are all stirred together, but you'd be wrong. It gets its name from the special prayer in the prayer book for that day, which says 'Stir up, we beseech Thee, O Lord, the will of thy faithful people.' So people probably got the idea to stir the pudding from the prayer!

## Traditions at every turn

One tradition says that a true Christmas pudding must be made of exactly thirteen ingredients, to represent Christ and his twelve disciples. Later in history, a charm – such as a silver sixpence – was added, to make it fourteen ingredients (because thirteen is an unlucky number) . . . which is why the charm itself is good luck to whoever finds it in his or her portion of pud.

In the days before decimalization (when all the UK coins changed), all sixpenny pieces – known as sixpences – were made of silver-coloured metal. When people refer to a 'silver sixpence', though, they mean one made from real silver.

The Victorians added many more silver charms to the mixture, each with their own special meaning. Find a ring in your portion and you'd find a sweetheart. Find an old thimble, and you'd remain an 'old maid' on your own. Just about every mouthful could have led to choking on something!

Every member of the family should stir the mixture from east to west, in honour of the three wise men. As they stir, they should make a wish which – if they told no one – might come true the following year.

*Now thrice welcome, Christmas,*
*Which brings us good cheer,*
*Mince pies and plum porridge,*
*Good ale and strong beer:*
*With pig, goose and capon,*
*The best that may be,*
*So well doth the weather*
*And our stomachs agree.*

From *Welcome Christmas*
– Anonymous, seventeenth century

# Robin Red Breast

WHY DO SO many Christmas cards have robins on them? Well, let's start with the obvious. We are a nation of bird lovers, and robins are some of the most attractive and colourful birds around in winter. Then there's the fact that their red breasts go well with red holly berries, Father Christmas's red suit and the red Royal Mail boxes in which most Christmas cards are posted.

Like so many things which can be explained in an everyday manner, stories have grown up around the little bird to give him a stronger connection to the festivities.

## The crown of thorns

When Christ was made to carry His cross, on the way to his crucifixion at Calvary, they put a crown of thorns on His head and mocked Him, calling Him 'King of the Jews'. The thorns scratched and dug into Christ's head, adding to His pain. The story goes that a plain brown bird flew on to Christ's head and tried to pull out the thorn most deeply embedded in His flesh. The bird was small and could only use his beak, but he pulled and pulled until the thorn came free. With it came a single drop of Christ's blood that stained the bird's breast bright red, before he flew away.

## Journey to England

A man named Joseph of Arimathea had Christ buried in his own tomb (*see page 29*). Later, he travelled to England and many legends grew up around him. One of the minor ones claims that the bird travelled with him. Thereafter, the bird's offspring were born with red breasts to remind the world of his act of kindness. And that is how robins came to live in England and explains their importance in the story of Christ . . . according to tradition, that is, not the Bible.

> *Art thou the bird whom man loves best,*
> *The pious bird with the scarlet breast,*
> > *Our little English Robin:*
> *The bird that comes about our doors*
> *When autumn winds are sobbing?*
> *The bird that by some name or other*
> *All men who know thee call their brother?*

From *The Redbreast Chasing the Butterfly*
– William Wordsworth (1770–1850)

# Christmas Cards

IT IS HARD to imagine Christmas without sending or receiving Christmas cards. Exchanging illustrated greetings on special occasions dates all the way back to the time of the Romans and ancient Egyptians.

In the fifteenth century, British engravers printed special Christmas pictures, often with New Year's (rather than Christmas) greetings beneath.

By early Victorian times, 'Christmas sheets' had become popular. These were hand-drawn pictures on single sheets of paper, with a space for the sender to add his or her name in the middle.

At that time, every 'well-to-do' person had calling cards, with his name printed on them. When visiting, he presented his card to the servant who answered the door. The servant would then take the card to the master or mistress of the house, to show who was hoping to see them.

If the master or mistress was out, the person could leave his calling card to show that he'd called. Come Christmas time, it became a tradition to add a printed Christmas verse or ditty to your calling card.

## The first true Christmas card

The first true Christmas card went on sale in 1843. It was the idea of a man named Henry Cole, who also had the idea for postage stamps with perforated edges. He had the whole thing designed by his friend John Callcott Horsley, printed in black and white by 'Jobbins of Warwick Court, Holborn' and then hand-coloured. The main picture was of a family party, with panels of small pictures showing people giving 'alms' (money or goods) to the poor.

The message on the front read: 'A Merry

Christmas and a Happy New Year to You!', and the whole card was edged with ivy leaves growing around poles.

The cards went on sale at Felix Summerly's Home Treasury Office in Bond Street, London, at a shilling each. (In fact, 'Felix Summerly' was none other than Henry Cole himself!) That was a lot of money, but they still sold about 1,000, and each fitted neatly into an envelope.

Envelopes were still a fairly new invention. Before they came along, letters were simply sealed down and the address written on the front.

Now that envelopes were established and the penny post – introduced in 1840 – meant that any letter or card would be delivered anywhere in Britain for a penny, Christmas cards were an instant hit. By 1880, so many cards were being sent, the Royal Mail first issued their now annual request: *Post early for Christmas.*

## More and more amazing

As time went by, cards became more and more elaborate and the verses inside became longer and cleverer. Some Victorian Christmas cards folded out into amazing three-dimensional scenes (like the very best pop-up books today.) Some used fabulous paper-engineering techniques, where opening a card could even make a character appear to 'climb out'! Queen Mary, the grandmother of Queen Elizabeth II, collected Christmas cards. These were donated to the British Museum in 1950, where they can be seen today.

> *I am a poor man, but I would gladly give ten shillings to find out who sent me the insulting Christmas card I received this morning.*
>
> From *The Diary of a Nobody* (1892)
> – George and Weedon Grossmith

# Christmas Carols

THE WORD 'CAROL' actually means a 'ring-dance': dancing in a circle. People used to dance in church as well as sing, often holding hands in a ring of people (sometimes around a pillar). Of course, this was banned by the Puritans like everything else that might have seemed too much like fun and not enough about prayer.

The person attributed with beginning the first true Christmas carols was St Francis of Assisi, who was born in the twelfth century. Assisi was in what is now Italy and it's from there that the carol spread – simple

Christmas songs full of good cheer and merry spirit.

A different type of carol, known as 'Nowells', then came into being. They started in France.

## Dividing them up

Today, a Christmas carol is probably best defined as a religious song – relating in some way to Christmas, of course – which is less formal than a hymn, though a few slip through this net. Carols have been divided into four kinds: jolly ones (such as *Ding Dong Merrily on High* and *Deck the Halls*), serious ones (such as *It Came Upon the Midnight Clear*), lullabies (the most famous of which must be *Away in a Manger* and *Silent Night*) and those which aren't really very religious at all (such as *Good King Wenceslas*).

## Who, where and when

The traditional period to sing carols was from St Thomas's Day (21 December) until the morning of Christmas Day. Different parts of the country – perhaps even each county – would have its own carols, or regional variations on a carol, called 'curls'. These weren't written down but learned by singing, passed down from generation to generation.

## The Boar's Head

Few carols appeared in print until the nineteenth century. The notable exception is a collection published in 1521. One of the oldest surviving carols is the *Boar's Head Carol*. Dating back to medieval times, this is still sung at The Queen's College, Oxford, as a boar's head is carried into the dining room for Christmas dinner.

## New traditions

One of the most famous carol services is 'The Festival of the Nine Lessons and Carols' held in King's College Chapel, Cambridge. It was first broadcast live over the radio in 1928 and such broadcasts have since become an annual tradition.

## Carol singing, door to door

Carol singing doesn't just take place in churches or chapels though. Many singers go door to door. Large, well-organized groups of singers often collect money for charities this way. Groups of one or two children who don't even know so much as a whole verse of a single carol often do it in the hope of getting a bit of extra pocket money . . . but where does the tradition come from? When carols were banned in churches, some people went from door to door, but this rather died out. Once again, we have the Victorians to thank for reviving the tradition, though they could equally have got the idea of house-to-house visits from the age-old tradition of wassailing.

*God rest ye merry, gentlemen,*
*Let nothing you dismay,*
*For Jesus Christ our Saviour*
*Was born upon this day,*
*To save us all from Satan's power*
*When we were gone astray.*
*O tidings of comfort and joy, comfort*
  *and joy*
*O tidings of comfort and joy.*

From *God Rest Ye Merry, Gentlemen*
– Traditional, seventeenth century

# Wassailing

WASSAIL WAS A drink, not a song. It was ale, nutmeg, honey and ginger. The 'ail' part of 'Wassail' has nothing to do with the ale in it, though.

The word 'wassail' comes from the Saxon 'wass hael', meaning 'to your health'. It was a Saxon custom that, at the start of each year, the lord of the manor would shout this greeting. The assembled members of his household would reply 'drinc hael', meaning 'drink and be healthy'. The lord would then drink from a large wooden bowl, which would then be passed on to the next most important person and so on, until everyone in the manor had had a taste.

## From door to door

As time went on, and people stopped living in their lord's house or castle, the peasants carried on the tradition by visiting the big houses to be given wassail at the New Year. They would take an empty wassailing bowl from door to door and beg for food and drink to fill it. This became called the wassail cup and it was traditional for wassailers to sing for their food and drink.

## Drink a toast

As well as wassail, people were often given small pieces of toast to float on the top of their mixture. The first wassailer then took a piece, wished everyone good cheer, chewed it, and washed it down with a swig of wassail, before passing it on to the next wassailer. This is where the term 'to drink a toast' comes from. By the time the wassailers had visited the last house of the night, they were probably getting rather loud and less tuneful. Drinking too much wassail has that effect on people!

## Other ways of wassailing

It was around Christmas time that wassailers might 'bless the apple orchards' to be sure of a good crop the next year. This involved meeting at dusk, gathering around an apple tree and pouring cider on its roots. Then everyone would make as much noise as possible – banging saucepans, shouting, blowing horns, and the like – to ward off evil spirits. The wassailers would then go home and have a good drink!

Wassailing became more connected with the religious side of Christmas when the Vessel Cup ritual developed. This was when people would go from door to door with a box containing dolls of Christ as a child and the Virgin Mary. The box was beautifully decorated and the dolls beautifully dressed. A special ancient song was sung, sometimes called the *Withy Twig*. The wassailers would get a drink for their trouble. It's easy to see how the Victorians developed this into carol singing door to door.

> *We are not daily beggars, that beg*
> *from door to door,*
> *But we are neighbours' children*
> *whom you have seen before.*
> *Here we come a-wassailing, among*
> *the leaves so green,*
> *Here we come a-wandering, so fair*
> *to be seen.*

From *Here We Come A-Wassailing*
– Traditional, Yorkshire

# Christmas Crackers

CRACKERS OF THE type that two people pull with a 'bang' to break open, to reveal a novelty, joke and paper hat – rather than those dried biscuits people eat with cheese – have been a part of the British Christmas for over 160 years. They're only now beginning to catch on in America.

A man named Tom Smith claimed to have invented the Christmas cracker. He owned a sweet shop and put little mottos on slips of paper inside sweet wrappers, with sugared almonds.

In 1846, he thought it might be an idea to put novelties and toys in wrappers, with the mottos, instead of sweets. And why not make the wrappers themselves more exciting, by having them pull apart?

It was then that he came up with the idea of the small 'bang' when the wrapping was pulled. (Some stories tell how he got the inspiration from watching a shower of sparks in a log fire.) Now he put all the elements together: the novelty and motto inside a pull-apart wrapper that opened with a bang. He'd invented the cracker!

## One slight problem

The slight problem with Tom Smith's version of events is that he invented his crackers in 1846 . . . and there's a story that mentions crackers which was published in 1841. That was five years before Smith's invention. It is, of course, quite possible that Smith came up with his idea without knowing anything about existing crackers. Maybe. Maybe not. One thing's for sure, though. It was his idea for including jokes as well as mottos . . . so you know who to blame for those dreadful jokes and groans at the end of Christmas dinner! By 1898,

Tom Smith's firm was the only one in the world making crackers and he produced over 13 million a year!

## Cracker etiquette

It used to be that, once pulled, whoever got the part of the cracker containing the novelty got to keep it. This often resulted in tears and some people ending up with nothing! Now it's usually agreed that a person gets to keep the contents of his or her cracker laid at his or her place or, if crossing arms and pulling a whole circle of crackers all around the table, you get to keep the contents of the cracker held in your right hand.

The more traditional time to pull crackers – if the suspense isn't killing you – is after the turkey and Christmas pudding, when people are eating nuts, chocolates and tangerines . . .

. . . and everyone, yes, everyone should remember to put on a paper hat!

# Why crowns?

Why are paper hats in crackers usually crown-shaped? Is it to represent the three kings (who were, more accurately, really three wise men)? No, not really, it's just that paper crowns are the easiest hat to make, because they don't need a top, and anyway, what kid doesn't like being a king or queen?

# The Christmas Crib

THE CHRISTMAS CRIB – models of Mary and Joseph, the shepherds, the three wise men, and a variety of animals gathered around the Baby Jesus in His manger – are now a common sight in churches, homes and even shopping centres. One of the first such models, simply showing the Virgin Mary holding the Baby Jesus, was placed in a church in Rome by Pope Gregory III (pope from AD 731 to 741).

One of the first Christmas cribs to include animals dates back to 1223 but was very different from our modern variety in two major respects. One real-life person played all the human parts (except for the Baby Jesus) and it used a real ox and an ass!

## To spread the word

It was the idea of St Francis of Assisi, who set up the scene on a hillside in what is now Italy, to teach the Christmas story. He was the man who played all the parts. Very few people could read and write in those days, and this was an excellent way of bringing the Christmas story alive for them. That year, the only wooden figure was the Christ Child in the manger (a hay-feeder for the animals).

The following year, the story was repeated, this time with a real baby. He was an orphan from a children's home. Year after year, the scene was recreated and the story told, each time with a different baby from the home. In a way, this could also be said to be the first Nativity Play, if it wasn't for the fact that one man played all the parts! (Nativity simply means the birth of Christ.)

## Beautiful carvings

In the fourteenth and fifteenth centuries, very fine examples of cribs containing carved figures began to appear. The setting varied from stables to caves to temples, and some were very elaborate indeed.

In more recent times, cribs have been built from snow, and there's even the extraordinary life-size underwater crib on the seabed, off Amalfi in Italy!

## Talking animals

A nativity scene without animals would somehow seem wrong today, but there's no mention of them in the Christmas story in the Bible (except for the shepherds looking after their sheep). If Christ was born in a stable – because there was no room in any of Bethlehem's inns – then it makes sense that some animals might have been there.

A tradition has grown up that the barnyard animals who saw the Baby Jesus that first Christmas found that they could speak. Thereafter, every Christmas Eve the world over, barnyard animals can talk, but we humans shouldn't listen in on them; that would be bad manners and bad luck.

*The cattle are lowing, the Baby awakes,*
*But little Lord Jesus no crying He makes.*

From *Away in a Manger*
– Anonymous, nineteenth century, USA

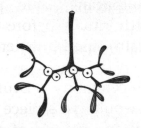

# Mistletoe

IF YOU STOP and think about it, kissing under the mistletoe is one of Christmas's strangest traditions. Like so many Christmas customs, the importance of mistletoe dates back to pre-Christian ceremonies.

According to Norse myth, Balder, the god of light, was killed by an arrow made from a thick stem of mistletoe, fired by his own blind brother (who was tricked into doing so). Balder's mother, the goddess Frigga, then seized the remaining mistletoe and planted it up a tree so that it would never touch the ground again and do harm to others.

## Druid ritual

The Druids (pagan Celtic priests who practised Earth rituals before Christianity reached Britain) used mistletoe in their ceremonies.

In one such ceremony, a Druid dressed in a white robe would cut a piece of mistletoe growing from the branch of an oak tree, using a golden sickle. It would be allowed to fall, to be caught in a white cloth. The ceremony then ended with two white bulls being sacrificed, and plenty of pagan prayer.

The plant – which has green leaves and white berries and only grows naturally in trees – is believed by many to have amazing healing powers and to bring good luck. The Celtic name for mistletoe is 'all-healer'.

## Whence came the kissing?

If mistletoe was seen as an 'all-healer' and a good luck charm, it wasn't a great leap in logic to imagine what it could do for a courting couple. It might bring a happy marriage with plenty of children. A tradition grew that, every time a young man plucked a berry from a mistletoe, still on the tree, he could kiss a girl. Once the berries ran out, so did the kisses.

With mistletoe in relatively short supply and so many homes now wanting some, a small sprig usually has to do, and its few berries are left where they are. The mistletoe is hung up to represent it growing on a tree and to keep it safely off the ground, which it must not touch. Those who stand beneath it can then kiss. Unlike holly and ivy, mistletoe is very rarely used to decorate the inside of churches!

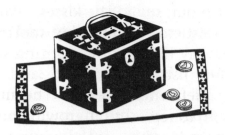

# Boxing Day

THE DAY AFTER Christmas Day is 'the Feast of St Stephen'. It was on this day that, according to the carol, Good King Wenceslas looked out and helped a poor peasant in the snow. Wenceslas was a real person, but a tenth-century prince and not a king. Also, he didn't do what the carol said he did. He did become a saint and a martyr (someone killed for their Christian beliefs), but the events in the carol were made up by the man who wrote it, John Neale. Many people imagine Good King Wenceslas to be an ancient carol, but it isn't. John Neale was a Victorian.

Another name for the day after Christmas Day is Boxing Day, though, if Christmas fell on a Saturday, Boxing Day used to be on the Monday and not the Sunday.

'Boxing' refers not to the sport but to boxes. This was the day that the alms boxes were opened in church and the money collected was given to the poor of the parish. This was called 'the dole of the Christmas box'. Over time, it became tradition to give a 'Christmas box' (a thank-you payment) to people who'd provided a service over the year, such as those who deliver newspapers and milk or take away your rubbish. Being a holiday, though, these 'thank-yous' are now rarely given out on Boxing Day itself.

# Christmas Presents

WHAT WOULD CHRISTMAS be without presents? The three wise men brought the Baby Jesus presents. Melchior brought gold, Caspar brought frankincense and Balthazar brought myrrh. Frankincense is a sweet-smelling gum from the *Boswellia* tree, used as an oil. Myrrh is also tree sap (from several types of *Commiphora* shrubs) used to make perfume. Along with gold, they were very expensive. (The wise men, or Magi, weren't given the title of the three kings until about 200 AD.)

Present-giving dates all the way back to the Roman sun festivals, but giving gifts at

Christmas was very rare in Britain. If presents were exchanged, it was usually to mark the beginning of a new year. This flourished in medieval times and in the sixteenth and seventeenth centuries. Money was given to the poor and needy at Christmas, but that was about it.

Then, perhaps influenced by Queen Victoria's German husband, Prince Albert, the giving of presents at Christmas – a custom in Germany – began to catch on, slowly, in the late 1840s. By the 1860s and 1870s, it was the New Year's gift that was unusual, and the giving and receiving of Christmas presents that was the 'done thing'.

# Twelfth Night

THERE IS SOME disagreement as to when Twelfth Night – when all your Christmas decorations should be down by – actually is. Popular opinion now seems to be that it's 5 January. With the Twelve Days of Christmas traditionally beginning the day *after* Christmas Day, however, I still think of it as 6 January.

The 6th of January is also called the Epiphany. In the western Christian Church, this commemorates the three wise men giving their gifts to the Baby Jesus. (In Germany, it is still known as Three Kings' Day.) In the eastern Christian Church, it commemorates Christ's baptism. In the east, Christmas Day was originally celebrated on 6 January.

## Foolish festivities

In England, people used to have parties on Twelfth Night and it was traditional to play practical jokes. These included tricks such as hiding live birds in an empty pie case, so that they flew away when your startled guests cut open the crust (as in the nursery rhyme *Sing a Song of Sixpence*).

Proper food included Twelfth cakes, dating as far back as the late fourteenth century. These contained a bean and those who found a bean in their slice became either the King or Queen of the Bean, and were put in charge of the night's entertainment. In many parts of Europe, Twelfth Night was the night for seeing off evil. This involved much noise, to scare away ghosts and spirits.

# Pantomimes

PANTOMIMES ARE A uniquely English form of Christmas entertainment. ('Oh no they're not!', 'Oh, yes they are!') with plenty of audience participation, old jokes, new songs and a magical atmosphere. There's no other theatre quite like it. It's been around in its modern form since the end of the eighteenth century, but pantomime's heyday was in the nineteenth century. In 1860, H. J. Byron wrote his version of *Aladdin*, which included Widow Twankey, the most famous of all pantomime dames – a man dressed as a woman!

# Scrooge

ONE OF THE most famous fictional characters associated with Christmas must be Ebenezer Scrooge, with his dismissive cry of 'Bah, humbug!' when it came to Christian charity.

Scrooge was a character in Charles Dickens's short book *A Christmas Carol*. After being visited by three ghosts, Scrooge becomes a changed man. He starts out mean and miserly and ends up full of goodwill to all. It was this book, first published in 1843 that did much to revive Britain's interest in all things Christmassy.

*. . . and it was always said of [Scrooge] that he knew how to keep Christmas well, if any man alive possessed the knowledge. May that be truly said of us, and all of us! And so, as Tiny Tim observed, God Bless Us, Every One!*

From *A Christmas Carol*
– Charles Dickens (1812–1870)

# Index

25 December 25, 1–2

Advent, 36, 37

Advent calendars, 37

boar's head, 39, 59

Boxing Day, 77–78

candles, 35–36

cards, 50, 53–56

carols, 57–61

chimneys, 14–15, 16

Christmas Day, 1–3, 24, 31, 36, 43, 81

Christmas Eve, 11, 12, 15, 27, 29, 30

crackers, 66–69

cranberries, 39–40

crib, 70–73

Cromwell, Oliver, 3, 30, 43, 46

Dickens, Charles, 3, 39, 84–85

Druids, 75

Epiphany, 81–82

fairies, 20–21

Father Christmas, 9–18, 44

frankincense, 79

gold, 79

goose, 39, 40, 49

hawthorn (flowering), 29–32

Hertha (goddess), 16

holly, 26–28

Holy Trinity, 6

ivy, 26–28

Joseph of Arimathea, 29–30, 51

King of the Bean, 82

manger, 70–71

mince pies, 43–44

mistletoe, 74–76

Moore, Clement
   Clarke, 12, 15, 19
myrrh, 79
Nativity Plays, 71
Norse legend, 17, 24,
   74
North Pole, 13
pantomimes, 83
presents, 2, 12,
   14–15, 16, 37,
   79–80, 81
Prince Albert, 7, 80
pudding, 45–49
Pudding King, 46
Puritans, 3, 30, 43, 46
Queen of the Bean, 82
Queen Victoria, 7, 80
reindeer, 11, 16,
   17–19
robins, 50–52
Romans, 1, 2, 79
roses, 33–34
Rudolph, 18

St Francis of Assisi,
   57, 71
Saint Nicholas, 9–10,
   14–15
Santa Claus see Father
   Christmas
Scrooge, 84–85
solstice, 1–2
sprouts, 41–42
star, 22
Stir-Up Sunday, 47–48
stockings, 14–15
talking animals,
   72–73
three wise men (the
   Magi), 22, 69, 79,
   81
trees, 5–8, 20–21, 22,
   35
turkeys, 38–40
Twelfth Night, 81–82
wassailing, 62–65
yule log, 23–25